CATS SET VII

TURKISH ANGORA CATS

Kristin Petrie
ABDO Publishing Company

visit us at
www.abdopublishing.com

Published by ABDO Publishing Company, PO Box 398166, Minneapolis, MN 55439. Copyright © 2014 by Abdo Consulting Group, Inc. International copyrights reserved in all countries. No part of this book may be reproduced in any form without written permission from the publisher. The Checkerboard Library™ is a trademark and logo of ABDO Publishing Company.

Printed in the United States of America, North Mankato, Minnesota.
052013
092013

♻ PRINTED ON RECYCLED PAPER

Cover Photo: Photo by Helmi Flick
Interior Photos: Alamy p. 7; Corbis p. 19; Glow Images pp. 16–17, 21; Photos by
    Helmi Flick pp. 5, 9, 13; iStockphoto p. 16; Superstock p. 15; Thinkstock pp. 11, 12

Editors: Rochelle Baltzer, Tamara L. Britton
Art Direction: Neil Klinepier

Library of Congress Control Number: 2013932664

Cataloging-in-Publication Data

Petrie, Kristin.
 Turkish angora cats / Kristin Petrie.
    p. cm. -- (Cats)
ISBN 978-1-61783-868-2
Includes bibliographical references and index.
1. Turkish angora cat--Juvenile literature.   I. Title.
636.8--dc23

2013932664

CONTENTS

Lions, Tigers, and Cats 4

Turkish Angora Cats 6

Qualities 8

Coat and Color 10

Size 12

Care 14

Feeding 16

Kittens 18

Buying a Kitten 20

Glossary 22

Web Sites 23

Index 24

LIONS, TIGERS, AND CATS

What do you think of when you think of a cat? Do you imagine a fearless lion stalking its prey? Or a fluffy pet sleeping on a sofa?

Mighty hunter or loving companion, all cats are members of the family **Felidae**. There are 37 species in this family. And long ago, they were all wild cats.

This changed when humans began settling in communities. Why? Humans stored food, which attracted **rodents**. To cats, the rodents were food!

Humans quickly realized the benefit of keeping cats. In this way, cats became **domesticated**. In time, humans began **breeding** cats to get ideal qualities.

However, **domestic** cats retained their natural instincts. So, they are both excellent hunters and fluffy pets! The Turkish Angora is a perfect example of this.

The Turkish Angora cat

Turkish Angora Cats

Historians believe the Turkish Angora originated in Ankara, Turkey. The first written record of the **breed** was in France in the 1500s. By the late 1800s, the breed was established in England.

However, by the early 1900s, the Turkish Angora was nearly extinct. The Turkish government recognized this as the loss of a national treasure. So, the Ankara Zoo began a program to save the breed.

In 1962, Walter and Liesa Grant brought a breeding pair of Turkish Angoras to the United States from the Ankara Zoo. These cats began the breed in the United States. The zoo sent a second pair to the Grants in 1966.

In 1968, white Turkish Angoras were recognized by the **Cat Fanciers' Association (CFA)**. In 1976, a Turkish Angora won the CFA Grand Champion award. Two years later, color-coated Turkish Angoras became eligible for this competition.

All CFA registered Turkish Angoras must be descendants of cats from the Ankara Zoo's breeding program.

QUALITIES

If cats had royalty, Turkish Angoras would be king and queen! These cats are graceful and elegant. Their long, silky hair and slender bodies give them a refined appearance.

Though thin, the Angora's body is muscular and **agile**. This can get them into trouble! Tightrope walking atop doors and along curtain rods allows the **breed** to oversee all activity below.

Turkish Angoras are active cats. This playful breed is easily entertained. Batting small objects to the floor is a favorite activity.

Turkish Angoras are lovable and adoring. They bond with their family and are also friendly to strangers. Many Angoras are eager to greet anyone who enters their domain.

In Turkey, the breed is known as the *Ankara kedisi*, or *Ankara cat*.

COAT AND COLOR

The Turkish Angora's coat is medium-long, soft, and silky. Its finely textured single coat does not **mat**. It lies close to the body, maintaining the **breed**'s slim **silhouette**.

The Ankara Zoo's breeding program focused on cats with pure white coats. It accepted only cats with blue or gold eyes.

For many years, breeders preferred these coat and eye colors. But today, other colors are accepted. Solid, calico, tabby and tortoiseshell coats are common.

Sometimes, cats with white coats and blue eyes can be deaf. Approximately half of these cats have a **genetic** defect that causes this condition. For this reason, Turkish Angoras with coats other than white have risen in popularity.

Some Turkish Angoras are "odd-eyed." This means one eye is gold and one is blue. In Turkey, odd-eyed cats are thought to be special cats.

SIZE

Turkish Angoras are medium-size cats. Males of this **breed** weigh between 7 and 11 pounds (3 and 5 kg). Females may be slightly smaller.

A slender neck holds a wedge-shaped head. The head is capped with erect ears that are wide at the base and pointed at the top. Just below the ears large, almond-shaped eyes slant slightly upward.

Turkish Angoras with white coats may no longer be exported from Turkey.

Their bodies are long and slender, with narrow hips and shoulders. Despite fine bones and trim bodies, these cats are muscular and athletic. Their long legs are also thin. The rear legs are shorter than the front legs. They end on round, dainty paws. A long tail is narrow at the tip and wider at the body. It is full and fluffy.

Ankara is Turkey's capital city. Until 1930, it was called Angora.

CARE

Turkish Angoras are generally healthy and hardy cats. However, like all cats, they need yearly visits to the veterinarian for checkups and **vaccines**. The doctor can also **spay** or **neuter** your Turkish Angora.

At home, you should brush your Turkish Angora's coat weekly. This will remove dead hair and promote new growth. An occasional bath will keep the coat clean and healthy, too.

Regular teeth brushing and claw trimming are also essential to a healthy cat. Brushing removes bacteria from the teeth. Short claws prevent unnecessary scratching of furniture and people.

Turkish Angoras may want to go outside.
But cats that stay indoors are healthier
and live longer.

FEEDING

Some cat **breeds** are calm and enjoy sleep more than play. Then there is the Turkish Angora! This breed is in constant motion.

Due to its active nature, the Turkish Angora needs a healthy diet. Protein, **carbohydrates**, and fats are all essential to growth and overall health.

High-quality cat foods are easy to find in pet food and grocery stores. These include dry, semimoist, and canned foods.

Dry cat food stays fresh the longest. It also helps clean kitty's teeth. Semimoist and canned foods have advantages, too. They are easier to **digest** than dry food. Whichever food you choose, don't forget to provide your cat with fresh water every day.

Angoras are very affectionate and love to show off!

KITTENS

After mating, a female Turkish Angora is **pregnant** for about 65 days. She can give birth to a **litter** as small as three kittens. But, she can have as many as eight kittens!

The kittens are born blind and deaf. They rely completely on their mother for all of their needs. After seven to ten days, they can see and hear. The kittens gain independence over the next nine to ten weeks.

Turkish Angoras are usually healthy. However, the **breed** can have health conditions. Kittens with Turkish Angora Ataxia cannot control their muscles. And, about half of the Turkish Angora population has a rare blood type. A kitten with a different blood type than its mother can be very sick.

These disorders are usually detected in the early weeks of life. For this reason, kittens should not be adopted until they are 16 weeks old. After this amount of time, healthy kittens are **socialized**, **vaccinated**, and ready for a new home.

Kittens drink milk from their mother until they are about five weeks old.

Buying a Kitten

Would you like to adopt a Turkish Angora? If so, the first step is to find a reputable **breeder**. Good breeders are dedicated to raising healthy and happy animals. They know the history of their cats and can offer a health guarantee.

Breeders want their cats to go to good homes! So, expect to answer questions about you and your lifestyle. If the breeder believes you are right for an Angora, you may be put on a waiting list.

While waiting, get ready for your new kitten. Buy supplies such as a **litter box**, a scratching post, and food. Next, prepare your home for a kitten. To this playful breed, all items are toys and all spaces are hiding spots! When you finally get your kitten, it will be a member of your family for 15 to 20 years.

Turkish Angoras are loving companions and are devoted to their owners.

GLOSSARY

agile - able to move quickly or easily.

breed - a group of animals sharing the same ancestors and appearance. A breeder is a person who raises animals. Raising animals is often called breeding them.

carbohydrate (cahr-boh-HEYE-drayt) - a substance made by plants, which serves as a major class of foods for animals. Sugar and starch are examples of carbohydrates.

Cat Fanciers' Association (CFA) - a group that sets the standards for judging all breeds of cats.

digest - to break down food into simpler substances the body can absorb.

domestic - tame, especially relating to animals.

Felidae (FEHL-uh-dee) - the scientific Latin name for the cat family. Members of this family are called felids. They include lions, tigers, leopards, jaguars, cougars, wildcats, lynx, cheetahs, and domestic cats.

genetic - of or relating to a branch of biology that deals with inherited features.

litter - all of the kittens born at one time to a mother cat.

litter box - a box filled with cat litter, which is similar to sand. Cats use litter boxes to bury their waste.

mat - to form into a tangled mass

neuter (NOO-tuhr) - to remove a ma
glands.

pregnant - having one or more babies grow
body.

rodent - any of several related animals that have
front teeth for gnawing. Common rodents include
squirrels, and beavers.

silhouette (sih-luh-WEHT) - a dark outline seen against a
lighter background.

socialize - to adapt an animal to behaving properly around
people or other animals in various settings.

spay - to remove a female animal's reproductive organs.

vaccine (vak-SEEN) - a shot given to prevent illness or
disease.

WEB SITES

To learn more about Turkish Angora cats, visit ABDO
Publishing Company online. Web sites about Turkish Angora
cats are featured on our Book Links page. These links are
routinely monitored and updated to provide the most current
information available.

www.abdopublishing.com

K

R
reproduction 18

S
scratching post 20
senses 10, 18
size 12
socialization 19
spay 14

T
tail 13
teeth 14, 17
toys 20
Turkey 6

U
United States 6

V
vaccines 14, 19
veterinarian 14

W
water 17

16,

, 7

20

claws 14
coat 7, 8, 10, 14
color 7, 10

E
ears 12
England 6
eyes 10, 12

F
Felidae (family) 4
food 16, 17, 20
France 6

L
legs 13
life span 20
litter box 20

N
neck 12
neuter 14

P
paws 13

le animal's reproductive

ing within the

arge

ice,